Mind
the
Gap

MIND

the

GAP

Poems

Atom Rush

Special thanks to Kevin Gardner, Benjamin Metzger, Shawn Capizzi, Andrew Phelps and Ethan Weinstein.

Atom Rush Press
Danbury CT
www.atomrush.art

Cover and layout design by Glen Edelstein, Hudson Valley Book Design
Edited by Lyn Hottes and Christina Monti
Introduction by Michael Dellert
Photography by Vic lorillo

ISBN: 979-8-218-87368-4 Paperback
ISBN: 979-8-218-87369-1 eBook

Printed in the United States of America
First Edition

This book is dedicated to Julia for her
support and trust in my art, which has
made our love flourish and grow.

Contents

Preface

Mind the Gap isn't just a collection — it's a through line. A body of work that stretches from the cracked sidewalks of youth to the long exhale of a poet still burning. Atom Rush — Tyler Keur, if you knew him back when we traded poems in dorm basements and diner booths — has always written like he had some urgency to survive. And in this book, he doesn't just survive. He documents the entire struggle: inspiration, collapse, redemption, relapse, revolt.

The structure here isn't marked by headings or sections, but it pulses with a deliberate rhythm. Atom told me himself: the first third is memory and momentum — the better-focused poems from our shared era, when writing was still the way out. You can feel it in "She Blocks the Sun," "Don't Walk," "Free Will in Brewster." These are poems that come from concrete places — college town stations, Brooklyn side streets, night drives through Connecticut. But they carry more than setting. They carry the charge of trying to live truthfully in a world that rewards detachment. They remember hunger, joy, confusion, and the electric sense that something was just beyond our reach.

The middle of the book shifts form — shorter poems, stream-of-consciousness turns, flashes of absurdism and dis-

sociation. "Rave Review," "Soul Warrior," "Reckoning" —
they operate like poetic telemetry. Less architecture, more
signal. You don't read them so much as get hit by them. It's
the space in which Atom lets language break apart a little —
not because it's lost, but because breaking is how it reconfig-
ures. Think of it as the glitchy middle of a jazz set, where the
beat unhooks and something stranger emerges.

Then comes the long breath: the final third. These are
the poems you carry with you. "Trench Madness," once
a standalone chapbook passed around in dog-eared cop-
ies, appears here re-situated as part of a broader arc. So
does "God Street Mechanics," "Messiah," "Social Ghost."
These pieces don't just reflect the world — they drag it
in, unvarnished. They are spiritual documents in the true
American mode: part prayer, part curse, part street sermon.
The sentences stretch, but never meander. Every breath is
accounted for. The poet has aged — not softened.

And that's the real tension here. Mind the Gap is not
nostalgia. It doesn't romanticize the damage. But it re-
members. It remembers why we started writing in the first
place — not to impress anyone, but because we were try-
ing to survive being alive. Because language was the last
honest currency we had.

The title is apt. There's a gap between who we were
and who we are, between what the world offers and what
the spirit needs. Atom doesn't bridge that gap. He sets it
on fire and writes in the light.

— *Michael E. Dellert*

Mind
the
Gap

She Blocks the Sun

She blocks the sun with her hand
knows what my mind is thinking
ghost ships halted and sinking
she blocks the sun with every rain
reminds me of fool's advice
love is not free
in this paradise.

Turning down the path
where are we
where are we
it's simple at best
sliding into a calm mess.

She blocks the sun with her hand
knows just where we're going
realizing with a smile
there is no way of knowing
she blocks the sun with her pain
lies down to rest
the sky denying
her soft request
the bridge decaying
this wasteland
of vertical straying
across blue masses
to construct the center
again

falling through the feeling in your hands
footprints in the sand
that make no sense.

Turning from the dead end
where are we
where are we
it's life blessed
among this sudden distress.

She blocks the sun with her hand
knows what my heart is making
shrugs me off
returns me to the race
she blocks the sun with her presence
shining lamp of a goddess
her resistance
strikes mutiny in rough hearts.

Turning from the dead end
where are we
where are we
it's reckless out west
slipping into a calm mess.

Society Furiosi

Oh comrades
Oh companions
can we make out these words in the dark
my tears are spilling out of this poetry
a shot of whiskey
the sour-tasting spirit of Coleridge
the air sweeps over hills
surrounding these sacred plains
we built them
in gentle whispers in merging passion
we fell out of the backyards of our youth
into the declarations of beauty
from the fire in our minds

Oh comrades
Oh companions
grab the reins of this chain and break free
we gave up on lies
from the voices in the dark
we grabbed a vision of penetration
in every wall levied
abused angels

Oh comrades
Oh companions
Oh saviors
Oh false captains
vomiting on the deck
sing with me below the mast

youth struggling
a revised image of rebellion
in a world unforgiving

Oh comrades
Oh companions
bear your words on my flesh
let me love even in the dim moonlight
shadows can illuminate the mind
we are destined
to walk in the footsteps of ancient wanderers
a common ground
where we process the narrow prayer of poetry
let us live in the spectre of broad view
let nothing be left to perceive
the last words in living sculpture

Oh comrades
Oh companions
grab the reins of your chain and break free
a torch-lit shelter
expressions and features of the dying flame
of a passion locked in the archives
of Blake, Keats, Whitman
reciting to the stars

Oh comrades
Oh companions
a mind not distracted
we held our spirit
steady through our emotions,
even death could not crack us

Don't Walk

You write alone
the synchronic rain
hitting the ground
unnoticed rooftops
basement garages
above the wind
we try to be noticed
a shard of light breaks

don't walk

You walk, are you right?
to settle a bet you lost last night
to wake and write from the corner
of your bed or his bed or her bed
high but alert
furiously creating
light comes over the page
distressed passenger
you ride the snake of road
into Sinai chapels
awake
bless the skyline
howl at the foul moon

don't walk

Working on my synthetic sensitivity
stiff back hot concrete
riverbank touching the tide

brick-faced building
holds the city together
midtown tunnel
Manhattan bound
the sky is turning
someone yells at Jagger
Carr running
like a flawless dagger
what kind of porn
do we feel like tonight

don't walk

Faces, hands, people
stopping the stopped
you want to crawl with this crowd
feel the desperation of being
alive with the vibe
speak of silence
writing while you smoke
the faces of the restaurant
don't ask what we are thinking
a woman strong on her guard
a man strung to the street
you ride this venom
across holes of road
into vacant buildings
awake
to find the sterilized structure of this world
everything in motion

eyes poised to desert emotion.

Free Will in Brewster

Get in the car
anticipate the roads with your eyes
don't forget to notice
people degrading each other
don't forget to call
she would be the first to see you
no glory when you get there.

Get in the car
he will only bite the roads
leave you shaped in his seat
don't forget to pray
for the next caution sign
she will be the first to say
no prize for first place.

Get in the car
only if you do first
stop stumbling around
with your packaged NY medicine
don't forget to mention
you left your identification
she will be the first to initiate modification
no police report written.

Get in the car
hands where I can see them
legs chained to the floor

pressed face for show
don't forget to amend your statement
to reflect what they found in your ashtray
she will be the first to revoke bail
no love at the end of this rope.

Purdy's, next stop Croton Falls
stand clear of the sliding doors
watch your step
mind the gap.
Croton Falls, next stop Brewster
the end of the line
mind the gap
mind the gap.

Get in the car
you paid the man
under the table
no pressure needed
an exercise in free will in Brewster, NY
railroad to change
pick and risk yourself
no one cares if you fail to create.

Mirror

When I penetrate that doorway
memories will flood into me
and dreams will surface.
I will feel the cold heat
from the old kerosene.

I will walk those curved stairs
to the attic, to my room.
I'll remember the birth
of all those blind kittens
crawling to the corner of my bed.
I'll remember death
in the wall by a sledgehammer.

When I fall through the cracks
that scarred my first sleep,
the nightmares that awakened me,
the pain that startled me,
seeing myself in the mirror.

I'll visualize all those
roses and morning glories
that bloomed and survived
my backyard landscape.

I will pick the sickly rose
and let the thorns
tear my hands with blood.

I'll explore the backyard.
All those weeds in the garden
haven't disappeared
and the path out back
will be hard to follow.

I don't have the empty step of a child.
I will lay the rose
next to the rotting apple tree
where I buried those blind kittens
when they learned to see.

When I'm done seeing myself again
in that mirror
that broke so many times.
I'll escape free of the past
and never go back.

Sober

Sober at midnight
with a half-empty bottle of wine in hand
looking out of a window
at the vast dimensions of land
with my falling and rising eyes
full of pain and pleasure.
My body trapped in this smoke-filled room
the scent of strawberry incense
covering the sweet perfume of marijuana
being smoked by the dramatic burnt-out poets
in the corner of the dark coffeehouse.

Whispers in the night, as a man with a shaved head
stands fully erect, with a blank stare,
fire coming out of his mouth and eyes
screaming his lyrics of social stability
and his broken poetry of the superior Aryan race.
A small regiment cheers him on
as many others fall silent, laughing to themselves,
and my mind wanders unaware of this place
out into the deserted countryside.

Through the farmhouses and barnyards
through the haystacks and manure fields
running with the windmills
air fast on my shoulder
invisible in the grass plains
hiding in this shadow of a field

11

exposing my paper wings
and their false hope
to reveal the whispering voices
of tall endless forgotten trees in the distance
through the curving streams
and deep winding forest with its confusing paths
running into empty staircases of hills and cliffs
where Roark lay silent and naked
cherishing the earth with a vision of himself
and I look at my reflection in the murky swamps
hoping I am not alone.

Through the skies so blue and endless
impossible to be clouded
with any other existence
but our own passion
through the distant pools
made from eternal rains
made from the commotion
and motion of ocean,
earth trembling with fear
through open windows and tinted windshields
this vision of obscure figures
hidden beyond our own immortal reins
through the air crisp and fresh
tickling our flesh with sensation and rebirth
calming our minds with patience and mirth
and making us sleep
through all the thunder
blinding us with flashes
of brilliance parading

in the dark outlines
of our own reflections
I am not alone.

Sober at midnight
no escape into the intoxication of nature
the coffeehouse now bare
except for a few stranded vagabonds
drinking coffee and mumbling to themselves
a girl sits on the stage
a dark and hidden figure
speaking soft poetry that makes me sleep
and my clutched hand
will not release this empty bottle.

Holding Up

Why don't you fess up,
instead you leave us to guess
which side of the tracks you are on
if your quiver collects a sum
hiding in a dark recess
feckless bloom in excess
nothing left to ravage
fracked by savages.

How are you holding up,
it is not right
that you still must fight
the sick guardians of the light
holding up
a government that cuts no slack
busy pinning us to the rack
because we all back black
against the villains of this night.

Have they confessed,
blamed the process
to amend their mess
before we all digress into negative stress
which side are we seeing
shadows chase away the sunrise
no positive janitor
to fix that temperature gauge
to stem this extended rage.

How are you holding up,
don't give up on the fight
to stand for what's right
against the sick guardians of the light
holding up
a cracked system in rewind
busy pitting us against the pack
we are not easily defined on sight
there are villains in this night.

We revise to survive,
the dismal echo that rewrites
no more self-disguise
displaced complacency
in this dizzy carousel
where our children whirl
oblivious to the fake world
time to blow off the stop
before we slip off this cold lonely rock.

How you are holding up,
not much wiser, only older
we must learn to lend a shoulder
or we all go asunder
holding up
a warped sense of sympathy
no substitute for empathy
no more hiding out on this color scheme
a grave for truth and dream.

Truth and Dream

ruler of love
measured in mountaintops
severed elegy
transmitted off generation
cloaked image
crucified in false damnation
chief of respect
in path and strength
a destiny at length
from letters of intimidation
to fists of rage
Birmingham to Selma
ancestral shackles
strip man shift blame

share the bread
fallen from the table

substance in truth
fixed as captive
bayonets on the bread lines
empty rides in Montgomery
weary motion in Washington
triumph oh heart
depleted master
triumph oh mind
forgive master
never forget

share the bread
fallen from the table

testament in sacrifice
scroll burns injustice
the righteous in muted song
no answer in Memphis
cut off
from the lost soul of Lincoln
tolerance divides
respect revives
he learned Gandhi
peace in himself

share our bread
fallen from the table

The Filling Station

I wanted to dream
that the world was empty
and that love had to fill it.

Atom Rush

Scattered and dissected by madness and machinery.
Two realms of an invincible sphere,
a feeling outside spiritual shelter
free and fragile but caught in a prison
before gripping reality alone.
Another feeling of mental collapse
insane and broken
knowing you're a wanderer of some new abyss
opposing forces to one mind.

Soul mixed with desertion and conception
and if you need jazz
I got jazz,
jazz in your burrows
jazz in your burials
our jazz cold and ragged
like an old religion
jazz echoing this bitter anthem
jazz for ten dollars
that will make your head spin.
Your mind opens to the crowd
dead and civilized.

Be a rush
laughing at your minor reservations
laughing at your rationalizations of rationale
smiling at your revolutions
smiling at your beautiful devices

feeding off your rage with innocent lies
crying at you sad poet
dreams now a mist faked over again and again
lying to you like a child
with an old broken toy played with over again and again
dying with your breath moist
on a burning cigarette
your eyes in fury like a skeleton on mescaline
your visions could never provide
a hint of salvation.

Be a rush
beaten down but not out
wet and torn, lost and abandoned
creating and destroying the chains of time
and their old curses and doghouses
in graveyards and playgrounds
killing time with broken fragments
of obsolete memories
cradling your sweaty face of faith
for eternal poetry
fearing no strangling of dreams
hearing you speak nightmares
whispering a redemption of anarchy
understanding a voice of philosophy.

I am serene
tasted in my lust
you're jazz in the night
like two flies shaking

anything she wants, anything she wants.
I am a rush limitless and absurd
slaughtered and digested
by madness and machinery.

Woodman

put him through the wringer again
skin his soul
till it bleeds a trail
for you to follow
run him through the meat grinder
release the lion out of his den
pin him for tonight's feast

hang the phoenix for a laugh
break his heart
till it bleeds a tract
for you to be hollow
your voodoo dolls
will not work on him this time

got her ringer on mute
his resurrection
no surprise
cause I burn
I am woodman
and I burn

put him through the wringer again
release his soul
till it sinks to a wail
for you to descend
run him through the meat grinder
release the lion out of his den
pin him for tonight's feast

mark the phoenix with form
break his heart again
till it bleeds a tract
for you to be hollow
for you to ascend
suspicious scholars of the solar bird
sun dogs refract light
reflect on spite
poet without crown

got her ringer on mute
his resurrection
no surprise
cause I burn
I am woodman
and I burn

Love Without Risk

Leaving my body
the heart heals, hurts
no more
no more hold on freedom
defy the badge of fearless authority.

Leaving my soul
the mind thinks, distracts
no more
no more safety in truth
deny the state of fear-driven loyalty.

Live in the vehicle
live for our soul
no more
no more love without risk.

Brooklyn

A skip through Brooklyn
shadow waiters
cast new light on old surroundings
into memory we restrain
over tacos and wine
the glisten of holy art.

A dream through Brooklyn
memories not meant
to hurt and love
at the same frequency
we connect to every block
every unit on this dynamic street.

A memory through Brooklyn
bathtubs scattered on the street
frozen roots
titled sad eyes
static traffic
leaving is living is learning.

A vision through Brooklyn
lives packed
rearranged to hold
the coma we breathe
our deadline for concept.

A levee through Brooklyn
extended selves in every window
keep a beat in these lowly lives
immersed in washed brains
new roots ready to burst
on scene, make an impact.

We soar through Brooklyn
faithful artists
trashed on the street
fabled roots
scribbled by hand
by the mad poet.

A siege in Brooklyn
merged under express thunder
trapped by one more light
a way to remember
everything that stood.

Take a Punch

First thought
seize the bottle from the drunken beast
to save the face of the beautiful bar maiden.
Second thought
secure the arena of the only bar
that I would stand up for in a fight.

Persuade with force the two inhabitants
abusing their presence
in the bar to leave.
Keg on my head
the confusion around the door
is it open or closed?

Flashes during the blackout
of his hand hitting my nose
the metamorphosis of my eyes
into the mad gleam of a barbarian
outside myself
strong.

I can take a punch.

The smooth way my fist rolled off his head.
Take it out of the bar
flesh not liquid

spilling beer is the worst injustice
you can do to a man
willing to stick up for a bar
desperate.

I can take a punch.

Wilderness

You control the room
a broom against liberal ideals
tracing trances in fruitless ideas
memory loss
false intoxication
endless stare
sickly smile scarred

a dark place
wilderness of mirrors
a sick twist
mirror of wilderness.

You are inhuman strength
built in pressure peaceful
convicted in concentration
unemotional self
the rosy chills of Doc Bryan
automatic writing
confetti-wrapped rain

a dark place
wilderness of mirrors
a hollow risk
mirror of wilderness.

A poet spy lies
banished from substance
robotic patsy
a polka-dot presence
in twisted CIA knots
red nail irritated
nonsensical gnats
rotating history
wilderness of mirrors
you are the dark place.

Stay Mobile

She is the caged dream in my mind
to see pain to recognize pain as old friend
come across memories
scraps of paper clever notes we write to ourselves
we gather thoughts from back of mind
unable to forget potent images of faces
drenched in rain
colorful sunglasses
rain makes every touch electric

stay mobile

The sound of highway
slips through cathedral forest
unconsciously aching
cigarette in empty port wine bottle
music unshaken by silence
make a pass at the stars
surrender naked body
quietly dismiss myself
to the noblest cause
paper houses on fire
indifferent to the emptiness
in mechanical structure
burn baby burn

stay mobile

We defend our right to congregate
when others find it easier to disassemble
fake love
forget another day
senile we stay
just seconds further
toward a way to say
easy to lie or rest

stay mobile

I want to let go of the wheel
and the way the road bends
away from me
the false sense of security that I feel
behind such machinery
I'm merely a spare part
I want to laugh
driving gives nervous freedom
turning away from back roads
to feel outside yourself
in the vertical dawn
we are down
to feel inside her self
captured thought in her voyeur world
feel nothing in routine
sadness you sustain
to pick up feet
before walking

You never taste enough like reality
your bottom lip
stale fantasy
your top lip
trembling stiff desertion
you never take enough reality
to bed with you
you save the integrity for easy money
you save the wicked grin for jealous survival
you're content only for stealth
or present involvement
in the grand slam and scheme of things
you never grow enough
for everyone to feed upon
part of the problem
taming what we have no control over

stay mobile

Uniting by a loading dock
highway speaking
the innermost feelings of rain on my skin
graffiti scattered and surrounded
the futile hostile back door of a bar
subtle runoff trickles down the building
cathedral highway calling me
speaking, surrounding thought with words
the sarcasm of all that
the simple idea
to let go on the street
to abandon body movement
when the music has just begun

stay mobile

Visual futility
smoke escaping like air
but visible
something magical
about holding it out a window
something thoughtless
to scream out when no one has spoken
a wind of mechanical motion
makes it seem distant
just one more feather to the wind

Hijacked into Meditation

Borrow my thoughts
if you will
you sit alone
in an immaculate diner
the sizzle of the grill
the clanking of silverware
the coffee-stained cup
left empty by your waitress.

The traffic outside
looks so familiar
you were here
when it thrived
the new faces
crowding your eyes
caressing your curiosity
and things were fixed.

Borrow my thoughts
if you will
alone for a moment
Billy Joel is coming clear
through the radio
waiting to inhale
a fresh piece of home
embrace these shops, streets,
woods, lakes, ponds,
your last stops before Eden

every song
from the past
like waking up
at night shivering
in a wet bed
and you are
an alien of passion
a fool for feelings
clear in mind
venturing into slumber.

Borrow my thoughts
if you must
my weary body a frame
an empty diner
cradled over the counter
burning cigarette not imagined
between fingers
sleep somehow now
justify life
falling apart
and my borrowed thoughts will be revealed.

Blind

One dream leaves
and another arrives

in the early dawn
where things are not recognizable

the last kiss is drained from your lips
a soul wanders inside you

words hollow when they are spoken
a scream in an empty container

heart in transition
a path that desires to be traveled
left to overgrow

once paved with hope
now narrow and dangerous
scattered with holes and cracks

dream declines to a whisper
somewhere in your mind

you wish to answer it
you say you will wait

all else is vacant
all else is vacant

no eyes can see what has made you blind.

Shackled

She is out there
speaking to the same glass
steamed and forgotten
I forgive our times
slay memories
because
she moves in dimension
a soft silhouette
that never sways just right

an awkward sad warmth
timeless
that never lands just right
across this busy highway
of lost burning souls
spiking the punch one last time
with mad glee
we customize in deleted frames
a weary seized tramp

shackled.

Funny How

I'll make sure
to leave a tip in heaven
large and generous.

If heaven has bars
when would they close
late or early?

Funny how
memory is selective
a way to build strength.

Do you remember
a sense of memory
when everything is eternal
comfort in mortality?

I hope Heaven has no aftereffects
no Vietnam flashbacks
no dirty politician hacks.
If I had a choice
I might choose Hell
who needs wings
when you have fire?

If Heaven has a good bartender
I will start a tab
a cute waitress,
I'll be sure to stiff her.

Mad Blues

Mad blues on the radio
a beat generation
that hitched a ride
a bebop lifestyle
on the balconies
in Greenwich Village
downtown San Francisco
giving donations
to the jazz in the streets.

Jazz mad blues
at the intersection
of spiritualism and realism
that ragged furniture
thrown on the street
a young beatnik
complains about weak coffee.

Mad blues on the radio
a beaten generation
a diluted trip
on a liquid acid culture high
on the bridge in Selma
sitting down in Washington
blooming flowers
in the barrels of your enemy.

Jazz mad blues
blurring the line
between suicide and consumption
to touch heaven
where Bird still blows his horn
and everyone dies at 27.

Awaken to jazz mad blues
you're the one
pouring through the open window
a beat generation
that beats themselves.

Very Little Sun

these days, things
accumulate like weather
moments will freeze
in slow train motion
the flash rivers we endure

these days, things
when you see, hear, listen
when you're vacant
in a smoked death
trapped, antique attic
a worn circuit

this daze
has very little sun
the insincerity
of sun rays
flattened by the trees

these days, things
have no meaning just memory
devoted to wandering
exhausted in wondering
the path you remember
or need to discover

these days, things
are seen with much disguise

seasons forget one another
we are the acceleration
of erosion in every
fall and rise
or need to realize

this daze
has very little sun
the insincerity
of sun rays
flattened by the trees

these days, things
dissolve seized remnants
dreams will sleep
in edged disturbance
rotating haze in inferior machine
the mindless voice we disband

these days, things
when you feel, know
the reasons
uncontrollable sadness
mechanical world of motion
a torn devotion

this daze
has very little sun
the insincerity
of sun rays
flattened by the trees

Rave Review

Did you invite them?
Seems too weird that
they're here.
Heard their poetry.
Did you?
Very obscene.

Soul Warrior

Got my lonely soul
bent to write
litany to old jazz
hits the pavement
an epic haunted with lost
hard echoing rain
lonely bearded
soul warrior
inside the minds
of others
outside pit bosses
shrieking at my dissidence.

The joke was on me
a punch line in reality
I'm no flunky
a soul warrior
the forgotten courier
a historical barrier
a soul warrior.

Lonely cradled soul warrior
he dreams of himself
locked in a cabin
surrounded by vinyl and whiskey
girls that dance to no music
lonely soul warrior
bent to the straightness of the world

suddenly and rash
we smoke it in a flash
pent-up resin for the masses.

The joke was on me
a punch line in reality
I'm no yuppie
I'm a dead ass violent hippie
a soul warrior
forgotten quarry
in this fake story.

Lonely soul warrior
scribbling away fancy writing
for the trench madness in us all.

God Street Mechanics

He is the poet crippled
indifferent
standing on a cliff
abused thoughts
running from the mountains
downward into a lush valley
entering as a whisper
into the womb
an outlaw of intimacy
a collector of lost sunsets
unaware malice.

He is the lasting menace
absorbed in silence
justified by an array of confusion
images melting into redemption
he puts his pen down to breathe
and justifies his malice.

You are just negative thoughts now
these horrid wishes
his deepest fantasies
his skin dry and callous
have you become a god
with no Jesus
a skeleton of jazz
where is your dark dream now.
Ha!

Scriptures of baptism
bury me
bury me
spit on our burning gravestones
the ground will sanctify us
my intensity
no souls will satisfy
my first resurrection
where are you
going mad in the moonlight.
Ha!
crucify this evil sickness
sermons, sermons, sermons.

I am a poet for
the puppets
the scars
the sands
that wrap this world
wrong this world
unaware malice.

I am a poet for
the robes
the ruts
the trenches
slithering in this world
this world of wires
of territories and the pissings
of government
this America of graveyards

of endless highways
in the dark
addiction of these nations
our world prey
to extinction
the distinction
of a poet
unaware malice.

The poet Charlie
learned to live
cooled with jazz
and jack Daniels
saxophone dreams
and thoughts poured
out of this doll.
Charlie played pool
in the smoke-filled sewer dives
he ran those curves real fast
he met diamonds
they were strange dust to him
the sacred lust
knowing these demons were gone.

In a cage suddenly
closets and claustrophobia
Charlie conscious
in the poet unconscious.

Serpents, serpents, serpents
in the snow
dancing in my face
laughing at my servant
my dependence
to survival
to a meaning crushed
stretched out in this vase
of god streets
running in the gutters
dirty equality
it must be our
cruel theories.
We revolve around
this demon street heroin
crash hard against
an agonizing shore
the ice breaks
our worlds tear apart
like symphonies
of battered whispers.

She carries a wooden Jesus
in her soul
like so many
spaceless conceptions of regret.
No security for the crystal
Sand castles in her mind
the outcome of changing dimensions
without your shadows
like a shower of dreams

raining the tears
of a lost chastity.
She carries the wooden Jesus
the virgin abortion
childhood scenery
a burning murmur in darkness
unaware malice.

Driving down god street
wind in my hair
wheel in my hand
eyes on the sky
drugs in my mind
souls on the street
walking, vanishing
into blind alleys
a raven in the sky penetrates this solitude.

Driving down god street
feeling like a sinner
he shrines the pavement
with his glance.

Civilized Automation

You are all concrete machines
with fuel thoughts and safety latches
always a little dangerous without instructions
and never without escape valves.

You run only to break down and search endlessly
like an addict
for naked oil and vain gas
to make you pure
to make you run smoothly
at this messy intersection.

You pollute the dirty snow
and empty every tide
with your exhaust
then see only decaying corpses around you
then you break, spilling out among us
we see your inner mechanisms sprawl before us
we are the madmen, who laugh,
walking out among these streets
seeing the vast hard faces of truth and experience
but violence cannot fulfill these angry stares
darkness veils but it cannot hide
submerged beings
we are laid to waste in these broken fragments
of a dark dream.

Hope won't make us strong enough
to fight the waves of downtown traffic
that has us backed up for miles
our horns can't move the other beings traveling
seeking some exit for a night's stay
in a cold motel
with no cable and carpeted floors
elevators that lead nowhere.

And bundled-up shadows walk every day
with a paper bag full of whatever they can afford
every day they walk like zombies
in this mechanical world
rotting their visions away
into melting flesh and mosquito eyes
no sight left in their abyss
a subtle hello is a dirty word
in this dying life of anonymous prayer.

Lights on a String

I stole her guitar
she wears her boots to bed.

She is my civil distraction
risks reaction
her soft appealing
end world extraction
she steals Wi-Fi and water
destroys this author.

She is hanging back
she does not want me to see her.

She dances the barren soul
sky of stars invisible
fog in technology
barrier in cruel judgment
fear the atom ramblings
buried words
rise to her static response.
She makes me sing the lyrics
before her song.

She is my uncivil dedication
carves attraction
her soft claiming
tender world extinction.
She deals Wi-Fi and water.

She is hanging back
she does not want me to see her.

Her smile catches shadow
harvests light in the bad lands
lingers truth in the mad lands
disguises fear in the sad lands
frees the oxygen from her trees
everything is the embryo of sky
a detached memory.

Free the oxygen from her trees.

Be Careful on That Ferris Wheel

Be careful on that Ferris wheel
it strikes back
she lies where the chairs sway
she will fake night with day
she will be ready to bury you on sight
she is going to steal
everything that is real
be careful on that Ferris wheel
she whispers to you
makes you sane
you are some swell dame
just don't care
if you take him home
sacrifice the whole
the only way a man can breathe
if he breaks the engine
the law that informs him
she dies where the fares lay
she will fake that she is awake
and be ready to cut you in line
she is going to make a deal
for everything that you feel
be careful on that Ferris wheel.

Scene Management

The mansion is packed
all the sacks are full
Falstaff drools at the sight
his tongue never misses a night
parties in the smorgasbord
hungers only for the marginal
must be the shadow we forgot
because we pick at this bone
seethes anger
under this relationship
unselfish and necessary
feeds on disdain
restrained under this pressure
sinks the basket for most
hits the home run for less
in this maze
of labyrinth and chaos
over this relationship
the tongues whisper
the bodies shift
in uncomfortable lust
and you must laugh
giving disorder
to this epiphany
torn

people change with pressure
they let go
the walls collapse

and vanish, narcissistic
but not without humor

people change with experience
they let go
relationships shatter
and fading addiction
is not without sarcasm

people change over the years
they forget what made them
who gave them depth
in a shallow tide.

Hard Barred

I am hard barred relentless
chasing tail under red light
banging heads into toilets
a nice piece in daze
edgy no feeling.

I am a hard bard
soft crucifix in the death hand
fibs pursue tales of ordinary madness
with disdain and fascination.

We are lost on the streets
waves crashing over the rails
no place for the water to recede
our actions unable to proceed
hard barred to everything eulogized
and revolutionized
I just beg and borrow or brag
a nice piece razed
thoughts rip across broken glass.

I am hard barred ruthless
revealing truth
writing history from the source
warped and honest.

I am a hard bard
who sees the best minds in delusion
find resolution in crime
time spent on the hustle
you taking notes sweetheart.

We are rusted on memory
entrenched insight
crashed on your floor couch
draining your supplies
no pages for words to retrograde
our images of lost beats renegade
hard barred to anything fastened
and flattened
I just speak and sing or see
documents burn under broken class.

I am hard barred Bukowski
prime to steal your cut
raiding madness
steaming up windows
a nice piece in daze
edgy no feeling.

Almost Believe

Beckon a galaxy to exist
contrast in chronic tendency
visionary creed we recite in hypocrisy
the primitive one says
let men draw quarters in rust breath
impulsive at hate, and to relate
Cooper William hysterical saint

let it bend
in gods and governments

almost believe.

Reckon a system to realize
contrast in lonely memory
why its brightness
continues to burn
without the capacity to learn
the primitive one states
why such savagery for land
for blood in disguise?
Pain in the cries of blind profit
Cayce Edgar bleary prophet

let them flee
those angels and aliens

almost believe.

Reflect a message to revive
contrast in hidden truths
why do they cry for religion
but scream in judgment
the primitive soul treads
transform rant into chant
Paine Thomas
liberty without restraint

let it seed
in prophets and junkies
in gods and governments

almost believe.

Rectify your safe ground
burns in line, treks on light
the primitive soul muses
absurd chances denied
where do you begin to make amends.

Generator

restore the power
men diligent and careful
such mastery
surgeons peeling layers off with a scythe
unlock my buried treasures
in overgrown bush

halo for the men
to return to light, power, restraint
children loose in the night
mothers hugging in the dark
children thrown from sleep
Monopoly by candle
the man with stern discourse
he's missing Sports Center
locked into sleeping early
with his wife
you know what darkness
can do to a man
he will disguise his breathing
they could be sheer gods tonight
if they were to reactivate
just a bit of light
strangers restricted walking their dogs

he whines just behind me
reality born to gentle confrontation

Concrete Mind

I've got more rips in me
than in my jeans
and more concrete in my mind
than any foundation or creed
this freedom within you
covering seduction with bitter suction
underneath moth shadow
solutions rage hollow
her words tire
shatter absent matter.

I've got more rips in me
than in my friends
and more disaster in my time
than any reaction can heed
the resolutions invisible
roped in corrosive garden
inner falsity blooms
in echoing night
shadows always follow
her pain to the gallows.

I've got more rips in me
than my Cobain-stained shirt
more cynicism in my line
than any scroll or tweet
this angst rolled blunt
missing whispers

clawing identity away
artifacts stagger memory
she needs to sow and mend
skeleton dreams.

I've got more rips in me
than in my jeans
and more concrete in my mind
than any foundation or creed
this extended mental landscape
question substance
feign reality
trap door for the insane
her anger contagious
strips all patience.

I've got more rips in me
than in any pain
by any means, this is going down
denied saturated notes
protective echelon
advised in confession.

Frisco

sun melting away
ocean surround sound
and this coast
unbelievable
for the ones in flight
may they die here
infinite unruly disturbance
now parts the clouds
like a knife to knight
unafraid of the ocean
a poet at the movies
looks through a window
at a beautiful creature
towels in hand
gracefully walking
to the other end
of this immense maze
the sound of facility
the steam of wet fantasy
the sound of gentle plains
between sun and cloud
the sound of ancient trains
this beautiful woman
captures and controls
every curve and angle
his sight deflected
by neck-high
it is ivory sculpture

the way the sheets never stay on the bed

Broken Government

I got a broken nose
cut down, jointed bone
I will not go down this round.

In wrecked noise
acute to sound
distinct in disruption
for lines not secure
scattered by comedy
in leisure and soft design.

I got a broken nose
jointed down, shuttered bone
I am not going down next round.

In exhausted fall
against weighted incline
the pranksters
haunt in the wild
in every split head
split mind
spinning atoms for all
dodging crowds that blend easy
banishing carousels to free gods
seeing a heart of darkness
wrapped around by fanatics
every wire transmitted
across trapped liberty

rotten
reading to expose
the madness of writing
realizing the seams
of dreams are without matter
resurrected atom.

We got a broken government
shut down, stripped of sound
contempt to destroy everyone around.

In spliff inferno
I am woodman and I burn too
we come so close
for peace and justice
that never meet.

Ferguson Prorated

If you close your eyes long enough
you see what you want to see.

No Legs

I met a great lady today. She had brown hair and blue
eyes. I asked her for directions at the stoplight in the
middle of town and she gave them to me. When my eyes
met hers I was astonished at their beauty and asked her
if she would like to have a drink with me. Next thing I
knew we were drinking and talking and laughing.
She was a secretary downtown in a small two-man firm
that sold motors. I told her I was a garbage man and she
looked quietly embarrassed. I love putting people on the
spot.
Once we were over the quick silence we continued
talking on about family, hopes and past relationships.
When we got to past relationships I was scared to tell her
about Judy, so I didn't mention it. She confessed that she
was engaged a few years back but couldn't go through
with it. What I loved about her the most was the way her
eyes fluttered when she rambled on -- she was quite a
talker. The corners of her mouth were moist with pas-
sion. Her body firm, she wore a silky yellow sun dress,
her legs were exposed.
I never forget to wear my sunglasses. I left myself closed.
She looked more like a model than a secretary. Then it
occurred to me as it always does when I'm in the com-
pany of a beautiful woman -- is this real or does she
feel pity for my obvious handicap? Her eyes remained
hidden. It's hard to get close when there is so much pain
and you have no legs to run away.

Cataract

he has the eyes of a writer
keen and cagey
waiting for some threshold
to fall
the exhausted flowers
blooming
against a red sunset
more worlds to collide
with the power of the pen

he has the eyes of a writer
buried in his cataracts
a pupil of thought
a sight dilated
marked by his madness
cradled by his salvation
dimmed unwanted and hopeless
worthless to the wandering eye
set in his sculpture
the one inch of creation
denied by the unaware

as a writer he is tragic
no difference even if he didn't write

Edge

In between screams
you were popping pills
like it was going out of style
laughing in dream
a madman

watching a cigarette burn
powder on your nose
exploring your mind
during work hours

severed by poppy seeds
in a Wizard of Oz
or confused like Alice
where everyone is mad

one fairy tale dies
the page is turned
but you remain, haunting me
by your presence

a shadow not afraid to scream

on the brink of mankind's faith
anger
fist over fist
clutched
faded lights glimmer

under a dim moonlight
eyes blinded
nerves jittered
senses amplified
powerless towards destiny
pain camouflaged
chameleon of desire
driven farther away

tied up in a strangling reality
stranded on an island of isolation

silence screams softly
we sat around
full of the fear
that the madmen writers
speak about
almost always write about
the ones not afraid
to sing their jazz inside the crowd
going mad in the company of stars
unaware we watched

he sat motionless
upon that white rock
a symphony of stars
playing over his matted head
his body slouching
melting in the company of night
hands buried in regret
his tears
invisible scars

treading in open water
biting in contempt

the lava lamp transforms
atoms into atoms
breaking my mind
into flashbacks
of him
growing distant
coming apart
words diluted in alcohol
sweating in the corner
trapped like an animal
caged by his mad thoughts
translucent blue in his eyes
beauty but also sadness
his tears of laughter
in an evil world
hands bound
by a faith
though blood was always
on them
trying to strangle him
one hand on the Bible
one hand tight around
a bottle of one fifty-one
and I remember
his legs so still in the coffin

checkmate
pawn takes king

Optical Therapy

snow angels
amazed with sky

wooden fence

things taken for granted
quiet immunity in freedom

dusk came
lights eluded darkness
candles were kept
reclaimed by love
universal language
touching sentiment
shared crowd

they stroked a calm fire
marking milkmen and storytellers

Aesthetic

a theorem in calculation
postulates turning point
automates in reason
deductive intellect
beauty in axiom

it is best unlocked

an enigma in design
shuffles data
estimates reckoning
her wired algorithm
crisis in parallel

it is best locked

mad binary soul
tangled mess
left rotten

Softly She Breathes

sheets of rain
sifting dark concrete
angels flying in morbid patterns
dimming streetlights against
unfamiliar storm
suspended fireflies
disappearing from night
drowning in sour rain

softly she breathes
her cigarette words
escaping her mouth
invisible demons
in forbidden language
overcome all reality
empty substance clouds his imagination
mind racing
grasping images
of past moments
in jealous survival

she clings to her addiction
like stale heroism
trees shivering in the mist
lit up by cars
like zombies
headlights breaking
the cool moist air

a playground
ancient feelings
crucified by children chanting
conceived morals of gods
hollow droplets of pain
faraway windows opened
generating cries
deadly creatures of love
a dying art
nothing without words
the beach was abandoned
no lawn chairs or decapitated sand castles
no torn dreams of a child
a long pier sways quietly on the inspired tide
the frozen moon hangs in the stale air
tired and restless

she holds my hand
to scare away the demons
I taste her lips
wild with fire
soft as a razor blade
bleeding warm

Silent Campus

downshift to second
let it roll
through the rail track tunnel
sound your horn cowboy
no one stops

third to accelerate
leans to the circumference of force
in the way I press on the gas
she reacts
she purrs me into the windy grey night

what is left

the crawlers
fantasy and brutality
a war
machine made
to drive us mad

silent campus
voices that remark
we are this media
we succumb to reality murder

in three years
I will be sitting inside
a broken bus
writing
mad radio institution

Clay Figures

long thought forgotten
short thought revived
congregation disgusted
by all atrocities
shocked faces
molten sculpture
shallow graves marked by rain

grass is eternal

man, this grass is eternal
it keeps growing
under one divine law
higher than structure and technology
keen to the sense

it knows survival
it knows survival

man, I know survival

Loved Up

oh the wonder of substance
only the rushing stream
and the early bud
of this tree
on the top of this world

substance
makes me think
about covered wagons
a path with no destination
bum pioneer poets
you and me
the symmetry
of downward mobility
the upside-down
sense of movement

this is the drug kicking in

so devoid of worries
and fears
a sense of nature
without denial
open spaces tickling
your fingertips
the private eye
on your roof
swallowing your shelter

with a strained eye
the sound of traffic
the covered but lit
windows in the distance
do you make love in the light?
a coffin potato
looks aimless into the static of the television

the dynamic coolness
of city and stream
sound escapes nature
the traffic folds
into background
to block out the bitterness
of this porch prayer
witnessed by water and earth
moving under our feet

Bruised Bottle Drunk

he wants nature to recognize him
let him in on the secrets
of immortality
this underwater river
he swims in
this ring of rocks
these falls
hiding in corridor
shadow
peeks through
on grassy sun fields
islands with no names
bruised bottle drunk
last night
what a crowd
met someone
laying on her beach
he relates to nature
with his shirt off
walking stick in hand
careful
not to move too slow
hesitation
becomes a shower
to current

The Crying Mask

Severed rows in spaced faith
detained in protest
no one hears their voices
sad houses with closed blinds.
Cracks in the vase
as I shake fall flowers
his light given
his light taken
genuine strength and no faking
I can't cry with this mask on.

Detached storms remain in place
justice awoken not pain
no one sees their grave
sad houses with closed blinds.
He sheds his mortal shell
life staggers out
and I break awake spirits
smiles shine in this maze
the anchor in our race
I can't cry with this mask on.

Our procession divides
and says why
not so divine
we can leave it all behind.
Electrify sad houses with laughter
open the closed blinds

silence the pageant judgments
a singular ovation
to the plural calculation
our procession divides
and says why
not so divine we can leave it all behind.

Reckoning

This reckoning can't last
we will react
when our frequency is hacked
we crash the crazy diamonds
drive the headless shaman to ground.
Morrison in Mars,
nightmares with no stones.

This reckoning can't last
it begs us for less
cut and born to threads
in this unexhausted light
grab me a stick of fire
inside they can't get me.

This reckoning can't last
it begs for the time to pass
strength with every blow
judged by every crowd
we will react
when media forces realign
behind false minds.

This reckoning can't last
when is the next false flag
I can't read this rag
forget the truth I'm going stag
a generation with no center

children without mentors
or minders.

This reckoning can't last
it forgets us in the past
judges with every crowd
strengthened by every blow.

This reckoning can't last
words the backward clause
broken recluse law
abundant feed for the ones
that need shiny clothes
without warmth
to compensate
for no internal shine.

There is a reckoning
our frequency hacked
we don't react
dismissing fact.

The Happy Sellout

You created great art
they dragged it, kicking it into the street
and shot it
as a warning to others.

Reverie

a modern strangulation
stifled by moral agents
body platform
limited perception
recognize experience
adjust to demand
adapt to dispense

mad kid Kant
cracks your skull
burns your newspaper
for the sanctity of thought
one more fence whitewashed

a modern strangulation
mask obvious
poisoned introspective
justified denial
in corporations and governments
disguise altruistic movement
the face value of dissolution

mad kid Kant
kicks you down
burns lines of race
to build atrocity of rage
one more village in reclamation

a modern strangulation
cradles all points
its purpose reversed
dripped in ancient secrecy
Apache warrior bones
a crude display
born to the scenery

mad kid Kant
crackles the path
the brain is the seat of the soul
greed mediates the weak
to live outside the law you must be honest

Salvation in Rain

The banging of garbage cans thunder
roll them inside children.
The concrete steams, a white mist
rises in the dim shadow of late afternoon.
The trees lay silent
leaves saturated with cool rain.
The distant clouds turn grey
ready their screams
of early spring with the incoming storm.
The gardens are turning to shade
the lawns remain uncut
unaware of whispering premonitions.
The birds fly to shelter
with moist wings and soft cries.
The wind picks up
the world becomes stained
the endless dust
thrown amidst the dry confusion.

There is salvation in rain.

Danbury 3 a.m.

something about these empty streets
is deceiving
a rain steady across open canals
residential madness
invaluable commercial proximity
swallowed by brick fortress
an occasional gas station under shady tree line

Danbury three a.m.

a taste of heaven
throwing seductive half-smiles
from hurried pedestrians
who don't look up
the ones who remained at the bar
you know who you are
bartender groupies
walking a clever line
upstairs to one-room fantasies

Danbury three a.m.

a hope in art
to paint on afternoon signs
an eye through federal court
don't look up
the ones who track our progress
we don't know who you are

flowers falling down
balm forth moving
freedom in one way

Danbury three a.m.

a hobo hops on pharm train
to release desire
a warning to all liars
don't look up
we know who you are
the ones seized at the border
bonds to sell the sick
pictures in my mind

Danbury three a.m.

Social Ghost

We are social ghosts
creating journals in the desolate sunset
a void on auto-replenishment
a stake left rusted and driven into the earth
a stain in morphine and illusion.
We are social ghosts
aquatic deep in hazy moon
an umbrella for the falling down
a cleverly radicalized Nietzsche proverb
interaction in your absence
social ghouls what a mess
to haunt the rest
to cut at less
social ghosts what a regress
to the mass compressed
an invitation to inject.

We fill holes between the lines
jazz that bites hearts
felt through ruins
we scream at no more lines of communication
no more disabling flashes
no more enabling fascists
by the shining beasts bending down on Tompkins Square
pick yourself up
away from the vomits of stale beer
in the washed gutters
social ghouls what a mess

to haunt the rest
to cut at less
social ghosts what a regress
to the mass depressed
a comment on excess.

An uneasiness settles on the land
dried blood not forgotten
social ghost
tougher skin layer invincible
your absence breeds insulated masks
I can ride it out
vanishing on side streets
splitting atoms to explode
burning stocks in the market
I object to this theory
based on echo impressions
from the maps inside and outside
burying this steep in your minds incline
I will carry these reference points
etched in this desertion of memory.

Atoms Don't Matter

She is lying on the floor
I am lying to her
treating her like a substitute
for a drained heart.

She is lying on the floor
and I am kicking her
for wanting to fill an empty soul
with adoration.

I am lying to her soft face
shed of hard tears
creating ravines
creating canyons in her blue face.

She is falling to the floor
and I try to catch her
but not in this dream, Holden
you are a spectator
surrounded by the headline:
you let her through
only to cut her down.

I am lying to myself
that atoms really matter.

She is lying on the floor
a nervy ending
to a soft face
that only wanted love.

She is lying on the floor
her breathing drops
a deafening silence
neighbors unaware
checking their mail
but beneath this window fence
she is lying on the floor
no roommate present
only what God resents
a twisted frame seized
by loneliness and fear.

She is dying on the floor
a faithless ending
to a soft face
that only wanted to love.

I am lying to myself
that atoms really matter.

Funny Farm

I have this feeling that no one
knows me

Stick Houses

A thin disguise
barrier in dream
glazed by mint leaf
brittle pulse
cradles invasion
no changes can be erased before saving
her sharp needles always bleed.

A smell in pine barren
nature's menthol
gift-wrapped echelon
caged in laughter
in shaft of sickled vines
hanging shards
in lost holiday glow
her sharp needles always bleed.

A mean reprise
dream in barrier
anxiety shifts under embryo
from within the stick houses
her sharp needles warp from memory
disguised by art
for stakes built-in pain
don't go to sleep
the boogeyman is coming for you

Christmas lights cracked
to feeling
fostered
naked
to the third eye revealed.

Messiah

I've talked with the steel ghosts
in the translucent mist
in the Paterson smoked skyline
I've met the ocean where it dries away with the poison
of the Hudson near the graveyard of dead engines
I've walked through the cardboard towers
shelters for the maimed and disoriented
I've played with the seagulls that now are silent
under the white jungle
alive with the hunted and the hunters
I've seen the ground where thunder strikes
in our death we shall not sleep
awakened by the pain of our children's tears.

I've laughed at racist jokes
cried at the hate we buried
through years of casualties and coffins.
I've walked down streets in disgust
seen the neon lights
that crowds of people worship secretly.
I've carried lost children you say you never saw you
never heard you never bred you never bother anyway so
you sigh
I've listened to white jazz in the ghetto
sweet jazz in the suburbs
and found simple ignorance and neglect.
I've been imprisoned asleep in the sphere
that suffocates our feeling
but I have remembered my kind roots.

I've prayed with those wax gods atop many altars
our own minds plunging into the endless circle of religion.
I've known faith leads to salvation, salvation to death,
death to life, life to consciousness, consciousness to think-
ing, thinking to learning, learning to knowledge, knowledge
to sin, sin to faith.

A catholic is a protestant, is Ted Bundy strapped in
is a Christian, is Jim Baker
is a Jew, is David Koresh smoking hashish
is a Muslim, is Malcolm X imprisoned
is a Buddha, is Ginsberg on yage
is a Taoist, are modern angels with badges on crack.
I've taught my mind to accept mortality
but believe in immortality
I've examined the world's flesh, seen its skeleton
dissected and studied
the core of infinity and its injustice
I've felt the scream of agony
the hurt of prayer when God doesn't hear
I've thrown flowers on the grave of the atheist
and heard his last confessions
to the god he never saw
begging for comfort.

I've predicted the world will be dust
no more faith, no more ghosts, no more children,
no more prayer, no more confessions,
no more white jungles, no more poison,
only one kind of jazz and graves where we lay

death upon us
we alone
stripped of breath
become our own messiah.

Secluded Beach

Willows whisper in the shade of the absent moon
a beacon to creatures of love and lust
a candle melts lopsided
still glowing, still glowing, bleakly
where the light vanishes into shadow
where the tide draws back into the ocean
where we leave particles
that the water forgets to sift
with pain
we hold regret
shattered antique pictures
of bashing bearded souls
eroding the shore with verse
venturing to speak when all else is quiet.

This beach of uncertainty
where Whitman meets his lover for a swim
where rosaries fall and drown in its undertow
where solitude creeps up on me
leaves me, dissident
where poems strip the fruitful tree
and meet as piles of leaves
wet and deserted.

Ah, but is art so perfect?
Why must we demand the reader take notice
to lie alone on a dark plain
reciting these words

to throbbing earth with more heart
then the creatures must hear
such distant cries and howls
fading in the west.

Trench Madness

Sleep easy in the bunker
sleep quietly on your knees
shield the rocket red glare
away from precious eyes
sometimes it frightens me
to know
to see
people thrust against a wall
sleeping to the constant sounds
of our bomb ego
but we have New York
the city that never sleeps
the bombs will never cease.

Sleep easy in the bunker
sleep blind and naive to the painful world
a famine of human contact
blistered people
we are not people
but places in time
lost to the broken world
to a background
where the city wants to sleep
the bombs will never cease.

Sleep easy in the bunker
sleep cradled on the wall
where native words are written

we share to one another
during the mute commercials
to find
to devour
pushing religion like a drug
control what you want to hear
instant static we recognize
in a shelter or a vacuum
the bombs will never cease.

Sleep easy in the bunker
sleep cornered and divided from the painful world
unconfirmed reports
secrecy's been exploited
moments sitting at a light
railroad tracks
intersections collide
cars beating the yellow light
gentle acceleration
invincible
to the screams in distant lands
the bombs will never cease.

You sleep easy in your bunker
emotions suspended and linked to
faint soon-to-be ghosts
hiding to the alignment of civilization
retentions of a benign leader
he chooses apathy for the cure
it's all in the way

he wants to be remembered
the bombs will never cease.

We are bent sunflowers
conservatively placed
geographically challenged
in the weight of this world
strings extended across barren tracks
which way to eternity.

Run Down

First reaction
I struggle
to balance myself
against energized conveyance
the local authorities are frozen
I can't be run down.

Second reaction
I expose the drained curtain
the fabric of fading memory.

Run down in Danbury malaise
this mental fog is a phase
music circles the sky
my clavicle ready to die.

I was reckless with time
reciting poetry on a moving truck
we brawl with dreams
the ones that fall between the seams
shake the rearview mirror
The indifference of Bukowski
against the brain of Hemingway.

Run down in Danbury malaise
this mental fog is a phase
music circles the sky
my clavicle ready to die.

This is the end of my book
but the beginning of the conversation

www.ingramcontent.com/pod-product-compliance
Lightning Source LLC
Chambersburg PA
CBHW020413130626
46549CB00006B/2537